Beyond The Eco-Mind:
Enlightenment and Brain Integration
To Create An Ideal World

A New Paradigm for Social and
Environmental Change

Simi Summer, PhD

Acknowledgements

There is an ancient Vedic saying which explains that nothing is greater than the enlightened teacher - *Na guror adhikam.* The Vedic texts also reveal that the gifts one receives from the enlightened teacher are traditionally offered back in gratitude - *Tvadiyam vastu govinda tubhyam eva samarpaye.*

For this reason, I would like to acknowledge and dedicate this book to the ancient line of Vedic teachers who have protected and preserved the knowledge of the integration of life -100% material and 100% spiritual. Without these teachers, the knowledge of enlightenment, higher states of consciousness, and the development of full human potential would have been lost.

In my own experience, all problems in life arise from not taking recourse to the non-changing transcendental field of life located at the basis of everything in the manifest existence. The gift of these enlightened teachers is one of hope for the suffering humanity. They offer a formula which achieves the goal by turning on the light rather than fighting with darkness.

It is also traditional to honor both the teacher and one's parents as God. So I wish to express the deepest possible appreciation for the extreme devotion, love, and unbounded vision of my dear parents. Their faith in and support of their children has been unshakeable, invaluable, and unsurpassed. Their beautiful qualities of heart and mind stand as an inspiration to parents everywhere.

Finally, I wish to acknowledge the example of the many friends who are great leaders, spiritual luminaries, writers, artists, musicians, researchers, educators, and otherwise academically or publicly engaged, whose work and lives inspired me to go forward with the completion of this book.

It is said that we generally retain only a small portion of the knowledge and information we receive. For this reason, the reader is encouraged to read and re-read this short text until the message is clear.

The most precious resource of every nation is the total potential of the human mind.

Take action! Dive within to experience the transcendental field of life. Together we can create an ideal world!

Preface

I was introduced to the work of Frances Moore Lappé in 1972, when I received a copy of her groundbreaking book Diet for a Small Planet. I was attending an international training course in Spain and had recently adopted a vegetarian diet. I eagerly scanned the contents mistakenly thinking it was a New Age cookbook. As I noted the importance of plant-based complimentary protein, I was unfortunately oblivious to the fact that Dr. Lappé's carefully calculated mathematical thesis outlined an extremely simple and effective solution to address the problem of world hunger. It did not dawn on me until almost forty years later that she had offered a viable solution to one of the most pressing problems facing humanity today.

I rediscovered Diet for a Small Planet in 2014. The more recent review of the work caused me to bemoan the fact that if the world had carefully read and immediately acted upon the simple thesis presented in the book, by now we would have solved the problem of global famine and world hunger. As a result, the harmful effects of the Green Revolution and biotechnology might have been avoided. Furthermore, the predicted and desirable results of the global adoption of a plant-based diet might have been widely implemented - catalyzing improvements in global health, increased lifespan, dramatic reductions in greenhouse gas emissions, reductions in endangered species habitat degradation, and perhaps many more positive sociological, environmental, and ecological outcomes.

That same summer, I was also invited to an international women's conference organized by a group with a mission to create a better world. The conference had an environmental theme and I had a burning desire to invite the top woman environmentalist to speak. After intensively surfing the internet to review the choices, I concluded that Frances Moore Lappé was It! The theme of the conference was The World is As You Are: Culturing the Inner and Outer Environment to Realize Our Full Human Potential.

I was then quite fortunate to converse with a cordial young lady at Dr. Lappé's institute, but was disappointed to find that the author's busy book writing schedule would not allow for her to attend. However, her work was so compelling that in response I plunged headlong into a very thorough review of every video she had made, every article she had written, as well as a rapid review of a number of her books. Her innovative book EcoMind: Changing the Way We Think, to Create the World We Want really caught my attention.

I appreciated her heartfelt and introspective inquiry as to why we are not creating the world we want when the solutions seem to be right at hand and I wanted to offer Frances Moore Lappé my vision of the solution to the problems that she so eloquently posed. Having an unusual academic and professional background in consciousness-based education, Vedic administration, and Supreme Political Science as well as eight years in third party politics, I was sympathetic to Dr. Lappé's desire to reform the government. But deep inside I knew that the whole answer did not reside in trying to change the government or in making conscious changes in "the way we think" to create the world we want.

I had witnessed and participated in a number of large-scale "coherence creating" demonstration projects which employed the group dynamics of consciousness to create effective social change. Consequently, I knew from direct experience that at the basis of the astounding peer-reviewed and widely published studies on the sociological, economic, and environmental effects of these technologies was a phenomenon capable of producing a major shift in individual and collective consciousness.

These studies empirically verified the necessity of going beyond our normally experienced states of consciousness, i.e. waking, dreaming and sleeping, to experience physiologically unique higher states of consciousness. As such, the key to creating the world we really want seemed to me to belong to the unfoldment of full human potential as well as the measurable field of brain integration and total brain functioning which characterize the state of enlightenment.

Furthermore, I could not ignore the importance of "transcending" or going beyond the surface level of the mind as a means to achieve the author's goals. Prime in my experience was the fact that large groups engaged in these consciousness-based technologies seemed to produce miraculous, almost unexplainable external results - in war torn countries, in the weather, in the actions of heads of state, and in overall quality of life parameters.

I chose the title of the book so as to clearly contrast the Eco-Mind with the Enlightened-Mind and to give readers a vision of how in theory and practice it should be possible to create an ideal world. I must also mention that the text in this short book is in actuality a tribute to Frances Moore Lappé. It was written with sincere respect, admiration, and appreciation for her forward thinking, vision, and innovative insights. She continually offers extremely thoughtful and workable solutions to the problems of today's unsustainable world. She is a woman of great fortitude and courage who knows how to always remain a "lady." In a very delicate and refined manner she holds her ground firmly in ever-present defense of everything good in life, continually emerging as a leading voice for social change.

Thus, the principles brought out in this short text are in no way meant to undermine the thinking and writings of Dr. Lappé nor to replace the concepts brought out in her brilliant EcoMind book. This book instead seeks to provide as yet unspoken answers to her very sincere questions while taking her own solutions one step further to a more absolute level of fulfillment. She repeatedly asks throughout her book "Can we change our perceptual glasses or mental framework ... to find effective and immediate answers to the pressing problems of the human race?"

I feel that the answer cannot be anything other than an enthusiastic "Yes!" The only requirement is that a majority of people in the world open their hearts and minds, expand their vision, and adopt the consciousness-based approach to eco/environmental change. Adopting this approach does not require any specific change in thinking, beliefs, lifestyle, or cultural background. It is universally compatible, available to people in all walks of life everywhere on earth, readily accessible, and capable of effortlessly culturing thinking and action in tune with natural law as a result of the daily practice of these consciousness-based technologies.

May the world look beyond the material changing aspects of life and learn to transcend surface values of existence to find the answers humanity is seeking. In my direct experience, daily contact with the absolute, non-changing field of pure creative intelligence is the truly effective key to creating an ideal world, offering a universal and viable solution to many of the seemingly unsolvable problems facing humanity today.

Simi Summer, PhD April 2016

Introduction

At a time in history when women are actively developing innovative solutions to critical environmental problems, the ideas being promoted by Frances Moore Lappé have been widely embraced around the world. For more than forty years, Lappé has been a voice of social and environmental change. As a young student at the University of California at Berkeley she published her best-selling book *Diet for a Small Planet*. The book was the first to offer a practical solution to the problem of world hunger and proposed the global adoption of a plant-based diet to ensure enough food for all.

One of Lappé's newer books *EcoMind: Changing the Way We Think, to Create the World We Want* emphasizes that "the world is as we are" and highlights the importance of our "mental map" in perceiving and affecting our environment. Lappé's voice is one of hope for a new generation of socially and environmentally conscious citizens who wish to protect the planet and create a better world.

Beyond the Eco-Mind: Enlightenment and Brain Integration to Create an Ideal World was written to bring fulfillment to the worldview expressed by Frances Moore Lappé by offering a new paradigm for the positive evolution of the planet based on the development of individual and collective consciousness.

The Eco-Mind

According to Lappé, human beings are creatures of the mind who interpret experience though an unconscious "mental map" made up of the "big ideas" which orient one's life. She explains that the quality of our perception directly influences what we imagine to be possible. Describing the current collective consciousness, Lappé sees the human population as if trapped in a "mental map" that defeats its own purpose since is not aligned with human nature or with the wider laws of nature[1].

Lappé describes the planet as evolving in a direction that is not creating the world that we really want. The environment and the ecology are being destroyed, we have not solved major health, environmental, ecological, economic, and food security issues and yet she asserts that the solutions to these problems are right in front of us. Commenting that people feel "powerless" when it comes to putting these solutions into action, she refers to the power of our own ideas as well as the importance of having a coherent worldview. Her book asks the question: Can we remake our "mental map" and do it soon enough to solve the global problems we are now facing for future generations[2]?

Lappé sees the majority of the world problem-solvers as pessimists who are stuck in the hopelessness of our enormous ecological crisis and planetary challenges. In contrast, she sees herself as a "possibilist environmentalist" who firmly believes that we can turn the world's "environmental breakdown" into a "planetary breakthrough" by addressing the mindsets which are stopping each of us from solving these problems. These mindsets are described as what she calls "thought traps."

At the core is the premise of "lack" or "scarcity" - the notion that there is just not enough of anything - food, fuel, money, jobs, goods, or goodness which in turn creates a world of "separateness and scarcity" rather than a world of "unity, integration, and abundance.[3]" Culturing an "Eco-Mind," a mind which is established in all possibilities, maximum creativity, and alignment with nature, is Lappé's solution for the well-being of the planet. She urges readers to think like an "Eco-Mind" and reminds us that "we don't see things as they are, we see things as we are.[4]"

Although Lappé addresses major economic, political, and governmental issues surrounding many of the world's most pressing problems as related to the seven "thought traps," for the sake of this discussion we will consider the parallels between the Eco-Mind and the Enlightened-Mind from a consciousness-based perspective. The state of "enlightenment" will be offered as a model of a mind which can see the world through an unbounded "wide-angle lens" and a "mental map" characterized by brain integration and higher states of consciousness, able to effectively meet the ecological and environmental challenges of today's world.

Introducing the Science of Creative Intelligence

In 1971, as Lappé was publishing her first book, Maharishi Mahesh Yogi, considered the world's leading expert in the science and technologies of consciousness (Vedic Science) organized the First International Symposium on the Science of Creative Intelligence® held at the University of Massachusetts, Amherst, USA. Leading experts in all disciplines including systems theorist Buckminster Fuller and Nobel laureate Melvin Calvin assembled to present the newest concepts in every field of study. The conference had an interdisciplinary format in which each presentation was united by the common universal thread of a new science called the Science of Creative Intelligence (SCI).

The Science of Creative Intelligence is defined as the systematic study of the nature, range, and origin of pure creative intelligence, located at the basis of everything in existence and directly experienced in human awareness through the Transcendental Meditation® (TM) program. The SCI curriculum clarifies the role and function of this science by explaining that SCI can be logically explained, directly experienced, scientifically verified, artistically actualized, fully unfolded, and applied in all fields of life[5].

Although the scientific approach to gaining knowledge is universally based on the variability of the objective means of verification which depends directly on the state of consciousness of the observer - clear, alert, drowsy etc., the Eastern approach to gaining knowledge is understood to be a subjective means of gaining knowledge which transcends the object of knowledge and allows the knower to experience the source of knowledge at the basis of the thinking process. Gaining knowledge on this level is considered to be non-variable and non-changing.

The source of thinking, pure consciousness, has also been identified by modern physics as the unified field of all the laws of nature. To integrate the two approaches to gaining knowledge, objective and subjective, the Science of Creative Intelligence was introduced, supporting the understanding that knowledge is the togetherness of knower, known, and process of knowing. By unfolding the full knowledge of the knower (subjective knowledge) in addition to gaining knowledge of the known (objective knowledge) total knowledge can be gained[6].

In our normal daily experience we identify and define who we are by describing and experiencing the world around us in terms of the objects of perception. SCI defines this as object-based knowledge or "object-referral" knowledge. It is segmented and diversified, reflecting a worldview characterized by separation and diversity.

In contrast, subjective knowledge experienced on the level of transcendental consciousness is called "Self-referral." This means that the awareness is fully identified with the inner experience of the transcendental universal Self. This type of knowledge is unified and integrated, reflecting a worldview of unity and integration. It has nothing to do with collecting facts, information, or opinions.

Chart 1: Process of Gaining Knowledge

PROCESS OF GAINING KNOWLEDGE		
	OBJECT-REFERRAL	SELF-REFERRAL
APPROACH:	DIVERSIFIED	UNIFIED
INFORMATION:	SEGMENTED	INTEGRATED
WORLDVIEW:	SEPARATION DIVERSITY	INTEGRATION UNITY

Development of Consciousness and SCI
Remaking Our Mental Map

Fundamental to the principles of the Science of Creative Intelligence is the understanding that "knowledge is structured in consciousness" and "knowledge is different in different states of consciousness." When we talk about seeing the world through a specific "lens" or the kind of perceptual glasses we have on, e.g. cloudy or clear, this is a reflection of the quality of our consciousness and the state of consciousness we are in at any given time. The tiger of the dream state, for example, is not the same as the tiger of the waking state. Our perception of reality in deep sleep, where there is no experience, is entirely different from our perception of reality when we are actively engaged in the waking state whether writing a book or climbing a mountain. We see the world as we are. Knowledge of our world is structured in the quality of our consciousness and knowledge of both the objective and subjective levels of life is different depending on our state of consciousness.

15

Modern science delineates three major states of consciousness: waking, dreaming, and sleeping. Each has its own corresponding state of physiology as defined by EEG, oxygen consumption, cardiac output, biochemical changes, and other parameters. Daily experience of the three major states of consciousness is required for a normal state of physiological functioning. Equally, deprivation of any of the three major states of consciousness can lead to physical and mental imbalance. SCI introduces a simple technique which facilitates the direct experience of a unique fourth major state of consciousness, physiologically distinct from waking, dreaming, and sleeping[7].

The experience of the fourth state of consciousness is described as one in which the conscious mind settles down and experiences a state of "restful alertness." The mind is fully alert while the body experiences rest deeper than a full night's sleep. SCI calls this fourth fundamental state of consciousness "transcendental consciousness" or "pure consciousness," defining it as a quality of consciousness which transcends all thought and action. Pure consciousness, the field of pure creative intelligence deep within the mind, is said to be an unlimited reservoir of energy, creativity, and intelligence. It is infinite and unbounded in its nature. The Transcendental Meditation program is the practical technology of SCI which allows the mind to experience pure transcendental consciousness[8]. TM is practiced with eyes closed and is characterized by a unique set of physiological parameters.

Psychologists as early as William James have suggested that we use only a limited portion of the human mind[9]. The direct experience of pure transcendental consciousness addresses this concept by expanding the full potential of the mind. This effectively frees the mind from being "trapped" in a limited world view or non-ecological "mental map." This is because the individual is cosmic and as such the individual mind is capable of being fully aligned with the infinitely diverse laws of nature which structure the entire existence from the smallest particles to the far ends of the universe.

Conversely, Lappé's sees the human population as if trapped in a "mental map" that defeats its own purpose since is not aligned with human nature or with the wider laws of nature[10]. From the perspective of SCI, this is because the knowledge and experience of transcendental consciousness is missing.

SCI further explains that the nature of life is bliss and that the purpose of life is the expansion of happiness. Pure consciousness is universally available and the mind is naturally drawn inward to experience the charm of its own unbounded nature - transcendental pure creative intelligence. Coming out into activity, the mind becomes infused with the unlimited energy, creativity, and intelligence inherent in the transcendental field which then finds expression in the achievements of daily life. As individual life becomes more and more ideal, the qualities of an ideal society begin to be stabilized in the environment. SCI posits that in an ideal world the positive qualities of life will dominate giving rise to a social order characterized by "all good everywhere, non-good nowhere[11]." This parallels Lappé's description of an ideal life which is abundant in "goods and goodness."

The Relationship Between Consciousness and MatterUnity vs Separateness

The concept of a universal mind has been found to be consistent with scientific theory. Modern physics sees consciousness and matter as being intimately connected on the level of the transcendent. Leading theorists, including Sir James Jeans, have verified this concept and describe consciousness as a transcendental reality beyond space and time. According to Jeans "When we view ourselves in space and time, our consciousnesses are obviously the separate individuals of a particle-picture but when we pass beyond space and time, they may perhaps form ingredients of a single continuous stream of life[12]."

John Hagelin, known for his pioneering work in the area of unified field theory, identifies pure transcendental consciousness as the unified field of all the laws of nature, providing a conceptual link between the most recent advances in unified field theory and the precise descriptions of natural law as described by the ancient Vedic texts[13]. These findings suggest that the experience of the underlying field of pure consciousness is that one element which can address the "separateness and scarcity" in life that may stop us from thinking like an Eco-Mind. The experience of unbounded pure consciousness, the unlimited source of energy, creativity, and intelligence, brings abundance, integration, and unity to life rather than scarcity and separateness.

Research on Transcendental Meditation
Increased Internal Locus of Control, Self-Efficacy, and Field Independence

Lappé sees human beings as "doers" who love to solve problems and posits that central to our ability to solve problems is "how we perceive the challenge" or "how we frame the problem." She explains that "seeing" delivers our capacity to effectively deal with each problem and asks "Is there a way of perceiving the environmental crisis which allows us to take 'leaps of mind' and 'reframe our thinking' to solve these challenges for humankind or are each of us, as environmentalists, defeating our own ends?" And what about the pessimism which Lappé describes as characterizing the belief system of many of the environmental experts of our day[14]? We can consider a few important personality and cognitive traits commonly measured in psychological research to address these questions.

Locus of Control

In personality psychology, locus of control refers to the extent to which individuals believe that they can control events that affect them. A person's "locus" is conceptualized as either "internal," i.e. we believe that we can control our life or "external" meaning that we believe that our decisions and life are controlled by environmental factors which we cannot influence. Individuals with a high internal locus of control believe that events in their life derive primarily from their own actions[15].

Self-Efficacy

Self-efficacy is the extent or strength of one's belief in one's own ability to complete tasks and reach goals. This can be seen as the ability to persist and succeed with any task. High and low self-efficacy determine whether or not someone will choose to take on a challenging task or "write it off "as impossible. Self-efficacy has an influence on every area of human endeavor. By determining the beliefs that a person holds regarding his or her power to affect situations, self-efficacy strongly influences both the ability a person actually has to face challenges and the choices a person is most likely to make[16].

Field Independence

Cognitive style describes how the brain receives and processes information. Field independence defines the extent to which people are influenced by inner (field-independent) cues or environmental (field-dependent) cues to orient themselves in space. Field independence also defines the extent to which we make fine differentiations in the environment. It is considered a psychological trait associated with an internal locus of orientation or stable internal frame of reference. Field independent learning style, for example, is defined as the ability to separate details from the surrounding context. Subjectively one may not mind the external field while awareness is focused internally on the parts. From this perspective, field independence could be described as "reframing our thinking" as independent of influences in the environment[17].

More than 600 research studies conducted at over 250 independent research institutions around the world have clearly demonstrated the practical benefits of the TM program including increased internal locus of control, increased self-efficacy, increased field independence, greater speed and creativity in problem-solving ability, improved cognitive abilities, growth of IQ (at an age when IQ is not known to increase), as well as a spontaneous ability to live life more in tune with nature's laws. Research on the TM program has also verified increased moral maturity and high levels of self-actualization in TM practitioners. Effective in offering positive outcomes in cases of ADHD, post-traumatic stress disorder, high blood pressure, and heart disease, the TM program unfolds full mental potential[18, 19, 20].

We can conclude from this perspective that regular practice of the TM program may effectively address many of the "thought traps" cited by Lappé in her quest to promote the Eco-Mind. Increased internal locus of control empowers us and is the opposite of "powerlessness." Increased self-efficacy gives TM practitioners increased ability to persist and achieve the goal and a greater tendency to go the extra mile to solve the problems of the environment rather than "writing off the task as impossible." Self-efficacy also affects how we see the problem and is characterized by a mindset which is the opposite of pessimism. Self-efficacy gives the confidence necessary to solve difficult problems and achieve challenging goals.

Increased field independence in TM practitioners, sometimes described as the ability to maintain broad awareness while sharply focusing on details, is characterized by the experience of unbounded inner awareness which does not mind the external noise or obstacles in the environment and reflects the growth of a stable internal frame of reference. Increased field independence gives us the ability to "reframe our thinking" in a more evolutionary manner, independent of environmental influences. These positive changes in personality and cognitive style directly support the goals of the Eco-Mind model.

It is also important to note that the TM technique spontaneously produces the psychophysiological effects mentioned because it effortlessly facilitates the experience of "transcending" the thinking process. Other meditation and self-improvement techniques are able to make use of the surface level of the conscious mind, whereas the TM technique allows the awareness to go beyond the surface levels of the thinking process to experience pure awareness, the field of pure creative intelligence. This experience is correlated with increased EEG coherence as well as other unique physiological parameters[21].

SCI and the Environment
Why Problems Arise

SCI agrees with Lappé's theory that we have the ability to solve the world's problems and acknowledges each individual's ability to remodel the environment to create the world we want. According to SCI, we have a choice and our environment is a reflection of the choices that we make. SCI explains that every thought, word, and action influences everything in the environment. Our ability to produce a life-supporting effect on the environment is facilitated by culturing the ability to always think from a level of unbounded awareness which allows us to see the world through a "wide-angle lens" analogous to the "ecological lens" described by Lappé. With this expanded vision, the influence of our actions will be most life-supporting and evolutionary[22].

SCI defines the environment as reflecting the quality of our own life, acknowledging the interconnectedness of our own nature with the wider laws of nature. The influence that we radiate through all thought, speech, and action reaches the environment near and far. SCI also explains that all problems of the environment can be effectively addressed when we make use of our full creative intelligence.

If we already have the ability to create the environment we want, why do problems in life arise? According to the Science of Creative Intelligence, all problems arise because individuals are not able to act in a manner which is useful to themselves and simultaneously useful to the others. This is due to narrowness of vision, stress in the nervous system, and unmindfulness of the surroundings. The development of broadened awareness and a "wide-angle lens" is lacking. SCI also explains that if problems are found in life, education is responsible. This is because today's educational programs do not universally or effectively teach students how to act in accordance with natural law nor does the current standard curriculum provide a practical technique to systematically unfold the full creative potential and unbounded nature of the human mind[23].

SCI, which can be incorporated into the curriculum of any school without changing the existing curriculum, posits that by drawing on the unlimited energy, intelligence, and creativity available in the unbounded field of pure creative intelligence, every individual will be able fulfill their desires in a manner which simultaneously brings maximum good to themselves and maximum good to their environment. This is the basis for ideal citizenship - citizens who do not create problems for themselves, society, or their environment.

Thus, from the SCI perspective, the solution to all problems of the environment including floods, drought, hurricanes, global warming, famine, and food security is the growth of creative intelligence and "unbounded awareness" in individual life cultivated through the regular experience of the transcendental field of pure consciousness, the one unified field at the basis of the infinite diversity of the entire manifest creation.

Higher States of Consciousness and Brain Integration
Our Brain Creates the World We Want

Our brain is an interface between consciousness and matter. Experience changes both the brain and the pattern of connections between neurons. As a result we can create our own reality.

Every experience reinforces our worldview. The specific activities that we engage in use specific parts of the brain and every choice that we make is imprinted in the structure and functioning of the brain. This suggests that what we perceive and do today changes the brain for the future. Therefore, it is by choice that we determine the structure of the brain, which is an interface between us and the world around us[24].

Due to the way that our brain functions, we are embedded in a worldview that is shaped by our educational, cultural, ethical, and societal associations. This can make us blind to facts outside of our normal "day to day" mental paradigm. The understanding of how the brain functions supports Lappé's concern that our "mental map" makes us "blind" to the solutions that are right in front of us. Our environment, where we live, whether a rural or urban environment, climatic conditions, air quality, weather, poverty, and food security as well as crime, violence, and war all have an effect on the brain. When the challenges of the environment become too great, the brain "downshifts" into a stress response. The frontal executive area of the brain shuts down and the fight-or-flight response is triggered[25].

Stress has an effect on the way in which we perceive the world and on decision making. For example, theorists have suggested that environmental and political leaders who cannot see the solutions to the pressing problems of the world, may be caught in a pattern of partial use of the brain physiology caused by a stress reaction. It is as if they are viewing the world through glasses which are not really clean or clear. Because they are stuck in a fight-or-flight response, their brains fail to embrace the whole picture[26]. When limited non-total brain functioning dominates, there may be a greater tendency to engage in non-life supporting activities or make decisions which are not in tune with nature's laws causing harm to ourselves, our neighbors, our environment, and the world around us. Total brain functioning, characteristic of the Enlightened-Mind, is necessary to live and act fully in alignment with nature's laws. Research has also shown an improvement in "situation awareness capacity," executive judgment, and "decision making under stress" in TM practitioners, suggesting the use of the TM program as an effective modality for leaders in "high demand" situations[27].

We have seen that the process of transcending gives rise to a fourth state of consciousness distinct from waking, dreaming, and sleeping. Integration of transcendental consciousness with waking, dreaming, and sleeping is the prerequisite for the development of higher states of consciousness. The experience of higher states of consciousness is the basis of the Enlightened-Mind model and is characterized by use of the total brain. This highest pinnacle of human awareness and brain integration allows the brain to function in a holistic manner, free from stress. The Enlightened-Mind maintains unbounded awareness throughout the changing states of consciousness, without being overshadowed by stress or changing outer conditions. SCI posits that the stabilization of higher states of consciousness, which characterizes the Enlightened-Mind, enables us to perceive the whole picture and to engage in problem solving with an unbounded world view and "mental map" characterized by a wide-angle lens capable of making decisions fully in tune with nature's laws.

It is also important to note that although the physical structure of the brain is a classical reality, the atoms of our brain function in a manner which can be considered quantum mechanical[28]. The quantum mechanical model of the brain embraces the experience of pure consciousness which is beyond space and time and beyond the sense of material or changing events in life. Due to the quantum mechanical nature of the brain, human consciousness may be capable of generating "action at a distance" effects which are defined as a quantum process. This quantum mechanical model helps us to understand the far-reaching effects of brain functioning on social trends and the environment[29].

Brain Research on Transcendental Meditation:
The Importance of Consciousness-Based Education

EEG coherence measures brain wave activity generated by the whole brain. Higher levels of EEG coherence indicate greater integration of brain functioning. Extensive research on Transcendental Meditation has shown increased brain integration as verified by the following parameters: greater integration of cortical areas, use of hidden reserves of the brain, as well as high levels of EEG coherence during the practice of Transcendental

Meditation correlated with increased creativity, greater efficiency in learning new concepts, more principled moral reasoning, higher verbal intelligence (IQ), less neuroticism, increase in academic achievement, clearer experiences of transcendental consciousness, and greater neurological efficiency[30].

Chart 2: Increased Use of Hidden Brain Reserves

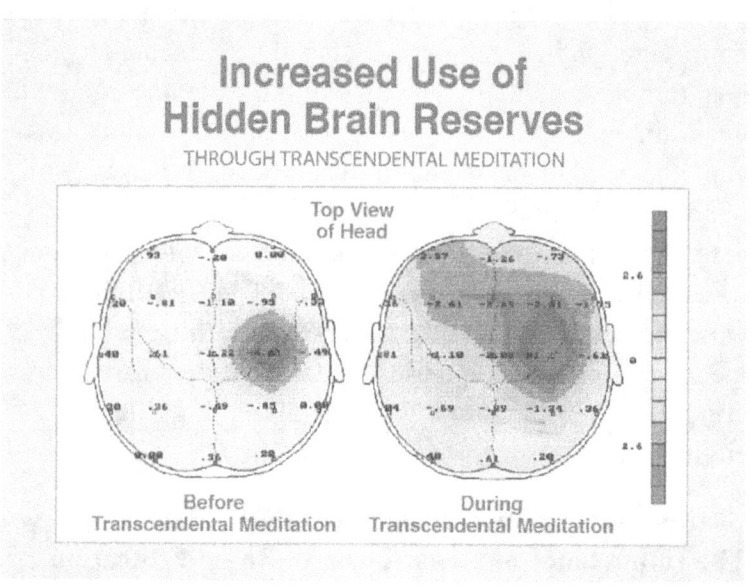

During the Transcendental Meditation Program sensory components of the brain's response to somatosensory stimuli are more widely distributed across the cortex, indicating greater participation of the whole brain in response to stimuli. *Program Abstracts of the International Symposium 'Consciousness and Brain'*; Russian Academy of Sciences, Moscow, p. 19, 1992.

EEG coherence during the experience of "transcending" reflects greater integration of diverse styles of brain functioning, greater activation of each brain hemisphere, and integration of diverse styles of brain functioning

28

associated with experiences of higher states of consciousness. Higher levels of integration of brain functioning are also associated with more integrated functioning of the physiology as a whole. Research has shown that individuals practicing the Transcendental Meditation program, in contrast to controls, show more rapid recovery of the autonomic nervous system from stress as measured by habituation of skin resistance responses. Transcendental Meditation program participants were also found to have a more stable physiological response to the stressful stimulus (fewer multiple responses) with fewer spontaneous skin resistance responses than control subjects (independent of the stressful stimulus). This is an indication of more stable and flexible functioning of the autonomic nervous system[31].

Many aspects of cognitive functioning have their basis in the growth of higher levels of brain functioning. Unfortunately, modern educational systems rely on a variety of teaching and curriculum approaches which do not develop these cognitive abilities after adolescence. This measurable lack of cognitive development suggests that the current system of education fails to unfold the full brain potential of each student. Research validates this concept by suggesting that the cognitive activities typically developed through education including reading, speaking, memorization, and recall as well as the study of specific categories of knowledge e.g. the study of art, science, philosophy, mathematics etc. all activate highly specific, localized areas of the brain rather than promoting a more holistic, integrated type of brain functioning.

Brain integration by definition is a quality of mind/brain development characterized by openness to learning and correlated with a quality of broad understanding which does not let negative emotions obstruct our ability to solve problems or achieve goals. Increased creativity, in the form of flexibility and originality, is also connected to whole brain functioning and psychological development. Because these parameters are vital for individual success, it is logical to conclude that optimizing brain functioning is an important priority for those designing the educational programs for students globally[32].

High levels of brain integration have been found in world class athletes, classical musicians, business leaders, and product development engineers who practice the TM program. TM practitioners also experience increased speed in decision making and information processing. These variables have been correlated with higher brain integration as measured by EEG as well as a unique integration of EEG associated with the experience of higher states of consciousness[33]. The research findings show greater integration of total brain functioning, the peripheral nervous system, and neuroendocrine processes[34].

Unfortunately, because modern education has failed to develop the total brain potential of every student, education everywhere is unable to realize its highest goals. The segmented approach to knowledge characterizing education today restricts the brain functioning to narrow channels of activity. Such restricted awareness may lead to problems, mistakes, and the inability to properly evaluate the environment, prohibiting each individual from acting in a manner that consistently favors progress, happiness, and the intelligent use of the environment.

Therefore, to fully answer the questions which Frances Moore Lappé poses in her *EcoMind* book, it is important to consider brain integration and the development of higher states of consciousness as an important component to meet her objectives to "create the world we want." This is because the Eco-Mind model as currently presented is a "waking state" model which relies on our "ideas" to solve the problems of the world. Lappé asks us to "change the way we think to create the world that we want." However changes in thinking, which take place on the surface level of the mind without transcending the thinking process, do not expand the conscious capacity of the mind, develop higher states of consciousness, or unfold full human potential beyond the current waking state paradigm.

Brain storming, creative problem-solving, and think tanks have become a popular means to address pressing social and environmental problems. Although highly creative minds will come up with innovative solutions reflecting high degrees of creative fluency and the ability to rapidly manifest creative ideas, the activity of creative problem-solving takes place on the surface level of the mind. To really expand the mind and go beyond the relative field of "ideas" to create the world we want, the importance of transcending and directly experiencing the source of thinking, the field of pure creative intelligence, cannot be overemphasized.

Fortunately, SCI offers the means to go beyond the "waking state" model described by Lappé by providing a technique to go beyond the surface levels of the mind where our ideas are normally appreciated. Over time, through regular experience of the field of transcendental pure creative intelligence, the conscious capacity of the mind becomes expanded so that every thought and idea begins to reflect the full range of the thinking process and the total potential of natural law. Rather than being stuck in isolated and fragmented laws of nature which in turn may be experienced as an isolated or fragmented approach to life, we are able to maintain the wide-angle lens characteristic of total brain functioning and the full potential of the human mind.

This is how higher states of consciousness begin to be lived in daily life. Pure creative intelligence, which is a field of pure consciousness, becomes stabilized. The mind becomes fully and permanently expanded so that one is living one's full potential. Thus, the Enlightened-Mind, characterized by higher states of consciousness and reflecting a quality of perception beyond waking, dreaming, and sleeping, naturally radiates a life-supporting influence to the environment. The positive influence generated by the Enlightened-Mind is then capable of spontaneously transforming the environment near and far. This has been verified by scientific research.

Chart 3: Beyond the Waking State of the Mind

Field of Pure Creative Intelligence

Levels of the Mind

Conscious Thinking Level
Waking State of the Mind Active Here
Ideas Are Appreciated on the Surface Level of the Mind
Limited Potential of the Mind

Finer Levels of the Thinking Process

•

•

•

•

Source of Thinking - Pure Transcendental Consciousness
Field of Pure Creative Intelligence
All Ideas Arise From Here
Full Potential of the Mind

Collective Consciousness and the Environment
Individual and Collective Enlightenment

We have seen that individual enlightenment, characterized by the Enlightened-Mind, is a model for personal development and unfoldment of full human potential and that a practical technique which allows the mind to transcend the conscious thinking level of the mind and experience the source of thinking is essential for the development of higher states of consciousness. But what happens when more than one person in the population begins to transcend and gain higher states of consciousness? What if a whole city or province or nation or even the entire world began to transcend twice a day? Can we create an enlightened collective consciousness on a city, provincial, national, and global level? How will this affect the environment and the world around us?

Every level of social organization is said to have an associated "collective consciousness" which is the sum total of the consciousness of all individuals in a society. Individual consciousness is said to be the basic unit of collective consciousness and each family, city, state, and nation has its own quality of consciousness. It is important to note that the quality of collective consciousness is a direct reflection of the level of consciousness of each of the individual members[35].

Although contemporary social theory sees human beings as being separate from one another, western philosophical thought describes the connections between us as existing on the level of consciousness. Modern psychology describes consciousness as "a field through which individuals may be fundamentally connected" suggesting that the brain reflects and transmits consciousness. William James described consciousness as a "transcendental infinite continuity underlying the phenomenal world[36]." Emile Durkheim, one of the founders of modern sociology, proposed that a "conscience" collective is the essence of the underlying social fabric unifying individuals in society. He described this "collective conscience" as the mind of society created when "the consciousness of the individuals instead of remaining isolated becomes grouped and combined[37]." The concept of coherent collective consciousness can also be seen as an extension of the phenomena of brain wave coherence as measured by EEG. When enough individual brains are coherent, through the superradiance effect as seen in lasers and other coherent quantum fields, the entire system becomes coherent.

According to SCI, the key to creating positive social change is to increase coherence in collective consciousness. Lack of coherence in collective consciousness is caused by violation of natural law. All occurrences of violence, negativity, conflict, crises, and problems in any society are simply the expression of the growth of stress and massive violation of nature's laws by the whole population. When the level of societal stress becomes sufficiently great, it bursts out into large-scale natural disasters such as famine, drought, earthquakes, and floods as well crime, accidents, environmental problems, poverty, violence, and war.

SCI emphasizes that the basis of individual and collective violation of natural law can be attributed to a deficiency in modern education because the prevailing educational system is not educating the population to spontaneously think and act in alignment with nature.

How Consciousness Affects the Environment
Action at a Distance

Modern physics posits a field theory of consciousness which states that nature is fundamentally composed of quantum fields that mediate "action at a distance." Although such phenomena have not been reliably observed within contemporary social research, they are now well accepted by the natural sciences. To understand these phenomena, physics developed the concept of abstract quantum fields. The basic understanding given by quantum theory is that everything in creation is the expression of fluctuations of underlying universal fields and that all bodies and processes are therefore connected at fundamental levels. This understanding embraces the world's current ecological worldview. Hagelin advances this understanding, proposing that the field of pure consciousness is the underlying unified field and that everything in life is connected on the level of consciousness[38]. The concept of quantum entanglement explains this further.

Quantum entanglement is defined as "a physical phenomenon that occurs when pairs or groups of particles are generated or interact in ways such that the quantum state of each particle cannot be described independently."

Research strongly supports the understanding that the universe admits interconnections that are not local. This means that "something which happens over here can be entwined with something that happens over there, even if nothing travels from here to there and even if there isn't enough time for anything, even light, to travel between the events.[39]"

Consequently, space cannot be thought of from the classical viewpoint. The concept of quantum entanglement asserts that "intervening space, regardless of how much there is, does not ensure that two objects are separate since quantum mechanics allows an entanglement, a kind of connection, to exist between them." According to quantum theory the quantum connection between two particles can exist even if they are on opposite sides of the universe. "From the standpoint of their entanglement, notwithstanding the many trillions of miles of space between them, it's as if they are right on top of each other[39]."

Research on the Transcendental Meditation program practically demonstrates these principles in a social research context, explaining how and why the individual and group practice of the TM program has a positive influence on the environment and how and why someone meditating in Boston can have a positive effect on people in Africa. By transcending and enlivening total brain functioning, we can access a field of infinite correlation which fully connects us with the same one fundamental field of consciousness, universally available to everyone, anywhere on earth. This explains how we can close our eyes and positively influence the environment at a distance i.e. we can innocently create social change on the level of non-doing. Consciousness is an omnipresent unified reality. Separateness is simply a notion.

Extensive peer reviewed research has found that the square root of 1% of a population experiencing transcendental consciousness through the Transcendental Meditation program creates coherence in collective consciousness, resolving conflict and improving the quality of life. As a result, negative quality of life variables, which could be considered sociological symptoms of a non-sustainable society, decrease. These negative social trends caused by collective violation of natural law include crime rate, accident rate, hospital admissions, air traffic fatalities, war deaths, and international conflict all of which have been found to significantly decrease statistically in proportion to the percentage of the population practicing the TM technique[40].

Sociological research on the Transcendental Meditation program has also shown changes in weather patterns during periods of very high coherence in collective consciousness. This was monitored when 7000 practitioners of the TM program gathered together in one location for a three week period during which time there were extreme cold temperatures correlated with the rise and fall of the number of TM practitioners. Subsequently, this extreme decrease in temperature was found to have a positive and balancing effect in nature[41]. Ten years later, when government ministers and the military in

Mozambique learned the TM technique, the war-torn, drought-stricken country began to experience political peace and much needed rainfall, signs of balance in nature[42]. Increased rainfall at a time of extreme drought was later seen in Australia due to a sufficient increase in the numbers practicing advanced TM programs together in a group in one location[43]. The number of advanced TM practitioners necessary to achieve these results followed a specific formula in proportion to the total population. These findings suggest that the TM technique may be a viable means to effectively create positive social and environmental change.

Living Democracy
Good Governance

Lappé ties her thesis to specific understandings regarding governance. She believes in a "living democracy" that upholds government which governs for the public good. Lappé suggests that only by "living democracy" can we effectively solve today's social and environmental crises[44].

According to SCI, government is governed by the collective consciousness of the people and government can only act according to the deserving ability of the people which in turn is determined by the degree of coherence in the collective consciousness[45]. When crime, war, and other violations of natural law dominate in society, an incoherent atmosphere is created in which it is difficult for national leaders to make positive and evolutionary decisions.

Conversely, when a sufficient percentage of the population practices the Transcendental Meditation program together in a group, collective consciousness becomes coherent and the government is positively affected. As a result, the public good is spontaneously lived in societal life. This has been demonstrated through content analysis research showing more positive actions and speech of heads of state[46] as well an increase in positive social variables such as improvements in the stock market in proportion to the size of the population and the size of the TM group practicing these technologies. Growth of the public good is further validated by research studies which found a decrease in negative social variables including crime rate, pollution, accident rate, unemployment, and hospital admissions as well as significant reductions in Okun's misery index (a measure of the quality of economic life) due to the collective group practice of the Transcendental Meditation program in significant proportion to the size of the population[47].

Thus we can see that the Science of Creative Intelligence fosters social change by handling individual and collective consciousness. By doing so, the nation begins to be governed by a unique phenomena known as "automation in administration." This innocent phenomena allows the coherent field effects of consciousness generated by the group practice of the TM program to positively influence the administration in a natural and evolutionary manner. As a result, the functioning of the government of any nation can become aligned with the perfect and orderly administration of the universe. Then national law will be administered by natural law.

When enlightened governmental functioning is achieved the administered (coherent collective consciousness of the entire population) administers the administration as much as the administration administers the administered (society as a whole). This is government for the people, by the people, reflective of the highest levels of coherence in collective consciousness. When maximum coherence is lived in individual and collective life then both the individual and the nation are capable of spontaneously "living democracy" and reflecting the highest aspirations of government. A sufficient number of individuals transcending twice a day can reliably produce this effect.

One final point with regard to government. It may be useful to consider that our brain can influence our ability to create a "living democracy." For example, studies on the neurocognitive correlates of political thought, specifically liberalism and conservatism, found that people with opposing political beliefs have a different make-up of grey matter as well as a difference in the size of various components of their brain structure[49]. These structural brain differences were found to have an effect on abstract thinking and brain processing.

The differences in political brains have also been measured using event-related potentials, a measure of the brain's response to stimuli[50]. This research suggests that total brain functioning and holistic brain integration may be an important characteristic of those individuals

41

possessing the unified political worldview and belief system which is required to uphold the public good, a living democracy, and the criterion for good governance set by Lappé.

Beyond the Eco-Mind
Enlightenment and Brain Integration
To Create an Ideal World

Solving the world's environmental problems requires increased creativity, intelligence, vision, and foresight as well as greater sensitivity to nature and how nature's laws function. Creating an environmentally balanced and ecologically sound world also requires a highly developed mind. From this perspective, the use of full creative potential is a necessity to facilitate socially and environmentally responsible solutions which do not violate the laws of nature, harm the environment, or damage the interests of anyone or anything around us.

Every action affects the entire cosmos. Our personal choices and "mental map" are important for the protection of the environment and the future of the planet. For our own health and well-being, we have to take immediate and sustainable steps to protect the world we live in for all future generations. Development of consciousness, brain integration, unfoldment of full human potential, and living the "Enlightened-Mind" can create the environmental and social change necessary for an enlightened world characterized by "all good everywhere and non-good nowhere."

Frances Moore Lappé asks: Can we remake our "mental map" and do it soon enough to solve the global problems we are now facing for all future generations? The answer from the SCI perspective is a resounding Yes! because consciousness is a field of all possibilities and on that level anything and everything is possible.

The world is as we are and we are masters of our own destiny and the destiny of the planet.

Enlightenment, characterized by total brain integration and cultivated through SCI and the TM program, is that missing element which can take us beyond today's "thought traps" and even beyond the Eco-Mind model. We can now embrace a new world of unity, integration, abundance, progress, and evolutionary change.

Meeting the urgent need for innovative and effective solutions to today's insolvable environmental and sociological problems, the Enlightened-Mind paradigm has been offered to facilitate the evolutionary sustainable development desired by Frances Moore Lappé.

By fulfilling the highest aspirations for ideal problem-free life on earth, this paradigm provides a very simple, universally accessible, and effective means to save the planet through consciousness-based social/eco/ environmental change.

Notes

[1] Lappé 2011, *EcoMind: Changing the Way We Think, to Create the World We Want*: 3.

[2] *Ibid:* 3 - 4, 10.

[3] *Ibid:* 11.

[4] *Ibid:* 2.

[5] Maharishi Mahesh Yogi 1972a, *SCI Teacher Training Course.*

[6] *Ibid*

[7] Wallace 1974, "Neurophysiology of enlightenment;" Alexander, Cranson, Boyer, & Orme-Johnson 1986, "A fourth state of consciousness beyond sleep, dreaming, and waking;" Jevning, Wallace, & Beidebach, "The physiology of meditation: A review. A wakeful hypometabolic integrated response."

[8] *Ibid*

[9] James 1908, *The Energies of Men*: 12.

[10] Lappé 2011, *EcoMind: Changing the Way We Think, to Create the World We Want*: 3.

[11] Maharishi Mahesh Yogi 1972, *SCI Teacher Training Course.*

[12] Jeans 1981, *Physics and Philosophy*: 204.

[13] Hagelin 1987, "Is consciousness the unified field? A field theorist's perspective."

[14] Lappé 2011, *EcoMind: Changing the Way We Think, to Create the World We Want*: xii.

[15] Rotter 1966, "Generalized expectancies for internal versus external control of reinforcement."

[16] Ormrod 2006, *Educational Psychology: Developing Learners;* Luszczynska & Schwarzer 2005, "Social cognitive theory."

[17] Witkin & Asch 1962, "Studies in space orientation: VI. Further experimentation on the orientation of the upright with displaced visual fields."

[18] Hjelle 1974, "Transcendental Meditation and psychological health."

[19] Jedraczak 1984, "The Transcendental Meditation and TM-Sidhi program and field independence;" Dillbeck, Raimondi, Assimakis, Rowe, & Orme-Johnson 1984, "The longitudinal effects of the MIU curriculum on intelligence and field independence."

[20] Retrieved from http://dl.globalgoodnews.com/pdf/research/
Bibliography_TM_Research_16_Apr_2014_Chalmers. *Scientific Research on Maharishi's Transcendental Meditation and TM-Sidhi Programme: Collected Papers, Volumes 1 -7.*

[21] Travis & Shear 2010, "Focused attention, open monitoring, and automatic Self-transcending: Categories to organize meditations from Vedic, Buddhist, and Chinese traditions."

[22] Maharishi Mahesh Yogi 1972b, *SCI and Environment.*

[23] *Ibid*

[24] Travis 2012, *Your Brain is a River Not a Rock*: 9, 38.

[25] *Ibid:* 149-150, 181, 186.

[26] *Ibid:* 156-157.

[27] Batorski 2012, "Developing situation awareness capacity to improve executive judgment and decision making under stress."

[28] Beck & Eccles 1992, "Quantum aspects of brain activity and the role of consciousness."

[29] Travis 2012, *Your Brain is a River Not a Rock*: 219 - 233.

[30] Lyubimov 1992, Programme abstracts of the international symposium 'Consciousness and Brain':19.

[31] Retrieved from http://dl.globalgoodnews.com/pdf/research/
Bibliography_TM_Research_16_Apr_2014_Chalmers. *Scientific Research on Maharishi's Transcendental Meditation and TM-Sidhi Programme: Collected Papers, Volumes 1 -7.*

[32] Lagrosen, Travis, & Lagrosen 2012, "Brain integration as a driver for QM success."

[33] Harung, Travis, et al 2011, "Higher psycho-physiological refinement in world-class Norwegian athletes: Brain measures of performance capacity."

[34] Retrieved from http://dl.globalgoodnews.com/pdf/research/
Bibliography_TM_Research_16_Apr_2014_Chalmers. *Scientific Research on Maharishi's Transcendental Meditation and TM-Sidhi Programme: Collected Papers, Volumes 1 -7.*

[35] Maharishi Mahesh Yogi 1990, *The Maharishi Effect: Creating Coherence in World Consciousness. Promoting Positive and Evolutionary Trends Throughout the World: Results of Scientific Research.*

[36] James 1898/1977, *Human Immortality: Two Supposed Objections to the Doctrine.*

[37] Durkheim 1893/1997. *The Division of Labor in Society:* 39, 60, 108.

[38] Hagelin 1987, "Is consciousness the unified field? A field theorist's perspective."

[39] Greene 2011, "Spooky action at a distance." Greene 2004, *The Fabric of the Cosmos*. Greene 2000, *The Elegant Universe. Superstrings, Hidden Dimensions, and the Quest for the Ultimate Theory*.

[40] Maharishi Mahesh Yogi (1990). *The Maharishi Effect: Creating Coherence in World Consciousness. Promoting Positive and Evolutionary Trends Throughout the World: Results of Scientific Research*.

[41] Rabinoff, Dillbeck, & Deissler 1981, "Effect of coherent collective consciousness on the weather;" Orme-Johnson, Cavanaugh, Alexander, Gelderloos, Dillbeck, Lanford, & Nader 1990, "The influence of the Maharishi Technology of the Unified Field on world events and global social indicators: The effects of the Taste of Utopia assembly."

[42] World Peace group: Mozambique transformation 1992.

[43] Invincible Australia course breaks 10 year drought cycle 2007. Retrieved from http://www.globalgoodnews.com/world-peace-a.html

[44] Lappé 2011, *EcoMind: Changing the Way We Think, to Create the World We Want*: 153, 154-156.

[45] Hagelin 2002, *Manual for a Perfect Government*.

[46] Maharishi Mahesh Yogi 1990, *The Maharishi Effect: Creating Coherence in World Consciousness. Promoting Positive and Evolutionary Trends Throughout the World: Results of Scientific Research*.

[47] Cavanaugh & King 1988, "Simultaneous transfer function analysis of Okun's misery index: Improvements in the economic quality of life through Maharishi's Vedic Science and Technology of Consciousness."

47

[48] Maharishi Mahesh Yogi 1992, *Maharishi's Absolute Theory of Government: Automation in Administration*: 22
[49] Amodio et, al 2007, "Neurocognitive correlates of liberalism and conservatism."
[50] Kanai et.al 2011, "Political orientations are correlated with brain structures in young adults."

References

Alexander, C. N., Alexander, V. K., Boyer, R. W., & Jedrczak, A. (1984).The subjective experience of higher states of consciousness and the Maharishi Technology of the Unified Field: Personality, cognitive, perceptual, and physiological correlates of growth to enlightenment. Harvard University, Cambridge, Massachusetts, U.S.A.; Maharishi International University, Fairfield, Iowa, U.S.A.; and MERU Research Institute, Mentmore, Buckinghamshire, England.

Alexander, C. N., Cranson, R. W., Boyer, R., & Orme-Johnson, D.W. (1986). A fourth state of consciousness beyond sleep, dreaming, and waking in J. Gackenbach (Ed.). *Sourcebook on sleep and dreams*. 282 -314. New York: Garland.

Alexander, C. N., Davies, J. L., Dixon, C. A., Dillbeck, M. C., Oetzel, R. M., Drucker, S. M., Muehlman, J. M., & Orme-Johnson, D. W. (1990). Growth of higher stages of consciousness: Maharishi's Vedic psychology of human development. in C. N. Alexander and E. J. Langer (Eds.), *Higher stages of human development: Perspectives on adult growth*. New York: Oxford University Press.

Alexander, C. N., Travis, F.T., Clayborne, M., & Rector, D. (1997). Maharishi Vedic Psychology brings fulfillment to the aspirations of twentieth-century psychology. *Modern Science and Vedic Science*, 7: 241-268.

Amodio, D.M., Jost, J. T., Master, S.L., & Yee, C. M. (2007). Neurocognitive correlates of liberalism and conservatism. *Nature Neuroscience*. 10(10): 1246-7.

Arden, J. B. (2010). *Rewire your brain.* New York: John Wiley.

Arenander, A. & Travis, F.T. (2004). Brain patterns of Self-awareness. In B. Beitman & J. Nair (Eds.), *Self-awareness deficits*. New York: W.W. Norton.

Assimakis, P. D. (1989). Change in the quality of life in Canada: Intervention studies of the effect of the Transcendental Meditation and TM-Sidhi program. Abstract published in *Dissertation Abstracts International* 50(5).

Batorski, M. M. (2012). *Developing situation awareness capacity to improve executive judgment and decision making under stress.* Pepperdine University. Retrieved from ProQuest Digital Dissertations, UMI Dissertations Publishing.

Beck, F. & Eccles, J. C. (1992). Quantum aspects of brain activity and the role of consciousness. *Proceedings of the National Academy of Science*. USA. 89(23), 11357-11361.

Boes, R., Harung, H.S., Travis, F., & Pensgaard, A.M. (2014). Mental and physical attributes defining world-class Norwegian athletes: Content analysis of interviews. *Scandinavian Journal of Medicine and Science in Sports*, 24: 422-427.

Borland, C. & Landrith III, G. S. (1976). Improved quality of life through the Transcendental Meditation program: Decreased crime rate. In *Scientific research on the Transcendental Meditation Programme: Collected papers, Volume 1.* Rheinweiler, Germany: Maharishi European Research University Press.

Cavanaugh, K. L. (1987). Time series analysis of US and Canadian inflation and unemployment: A test of a field-theoretic hypothesis. Presented at the Annual Meeting of the American Statistical Association, San Francisco, California, August 17-20, 1987 and published in *Proceedings of the American Statistical Association, Business and Economics Statistics Section.* Alexandria, Virginia: American Statistical Association, 799-804.

Cavanaugh, K. L. (1992). Maharishi's Vedic Science and Technology. The basis for economic development and world peace. *Modern Science and Vedic Science.*

Cavanaugh, K. L. & King, K. D. (1988). Simultaneous transfer function analysis of Okun's misery index: Improvements in the economic quality of life through Maharishi's Vedic Science and Technology of Consciousness. Paper presented at the Annual Meeting of the American Statistical Association, New Orleans, Louisiana, August 22-25, 1988. An abridged version of this paper appeared in *Proceedings of the American Statistical Association, Business and Economics Statistics Section*: 491-496.

Chalmers, R.A., Clements, G., Schenkluhn, H., & Weinless, M. (Eds.). (1989). *Scientific research on Maharishi's Transcendental Meditation and TM-Sidhi Programme: Collected papers, Volume 2.* Vlodrop, The Netherlands: MVU Press. (Papers 105–189).

Chalmers, R.A., Clements, G., Schenkluhn, H., & Weinless, M. (Eds.). (1989). *Scientific research on Maharishi's Transcendental Meditation and TM-Sidhi Programme: Collected papers, Volume 3.* Vlodrop, The Netherlands: MVU Press, 1989. (Papers 190–290).

Chalmers, R.A., Clements, G., Schenkluhn, H., & Weinless, M. (Eds.). (1989). *Scientific research on Maharishi's Transcendental Meditation and TM-Sidhi Programme: Collected papers, Volume 4.* Vlodrop, The Netherlands: MVU Press, 1989. (Papers 291–355).

Charles, G., Travis, F., & Smith, J. (2014). Policing and spirituality: Their impact on brain integration and consciousness. *Journal of Management, Spirituality, and Religion,* 1, 1-15.

D'Espagnat, B. (1979). The quantum theory and reality. *Scientific American,* 24, 158-181.

Dillbeck, M. C. (1988). The self-interacting dynamics of consciousness as the source of the creative process in nature and human life: The mechanics of individual intelligence arising from the field of cosmic intelligence, the Cosmic Psyche. *Modern Science and Vedic Science, 2* (3): 244-278.

Dillbeck, M. C. (1990). Test of a field theory of consciousness and social change: Time series analysis of participation in the TM-Sidhi program and reduction of violent death in the US. *Social Indicators Research,* 22: 399-418.

Dillbeck, M. C. (Ed.). (2011). *Scientific research on Maharishi's Transcendental Meditation and TM-Sidhi Programme: Collected papers, Volume 6.* Vlodrop, The Netherlands, MVU Press. (Papers 431–524).

Dillbeck, M. C., Banus, C. B., Polanzi, C., & Landrith III, G. S. (1988). Test of a field model of consciousness and social change: The Transcendental Meditation and TM-Sidhi program and decreased urban crime. *The Journal of Mind and Behavior,* 9, 457-486.

Dillbeck, M. C., Cavanaugh, K. L., Glenn, T., Orme-Johnson, D. W., & Mittlefehldt, V. (1987). Consciousness as a field: The Transcendental Meditation and TM-Sidhi program and changes in social indicators. *The Journal of Mind and Behavior,* 8(1): 67-104.

Dillbeck, M. C., Landrith III, G. S., & Orme-Johnson, D. W. (1981). The Transcendental Meditation program and crime rate change in a sample of forty-eight cities. *Journal of Crime and Justice,* 4: 25-45.

Dillbeck, M.C., Raimondi, D., Assimakis, P. D., Rowe, R., & Orme-Johnson, D.W. (1984). The longitudinal effects of the MIU curriculum on intelligence and field independence. Department of Psychology and Office of Evaluation, Maharishi International University, U.S.A.

Dodge, N. (2007). *The brain that changes itself.* New York: Penguin Books.

Dossey, L. (1989). *Recovering the soul: A scientific and spiritual search.* New York: Bantam Books.

Durkheim, E. (1893) (1997). *The division of labor in society.* Trans. W. D. Halls, New York: Free Press.

Eddington, A. (1984). *Defense of mysticism* in *quantum questions: Mystical writings of the world's great physicists.* K. Wilbur, (Ed.), Boston: New Science Library.

Gaylord C., Orme-Johnson D.W., & Travis F.T. (1989). The effects of the Transcendental Meditation technique and progressive muscle relaxation on EEG coherence, stress reactivity, and mental health in black adults. *International Journal of Neuroscience,* 46:77-86.

Gelderloos, P., Cavanaugh, K. L., & Davies, J. L. (1990). The dynamics of US-Soviet relations, 1979-1986: Effects of reducing social stress through the Transcendental Meditation and TM-Sidhi program. In *Proceedings of the American Statistical Association*, Alexandria, VA: American Statistical Association.

Gelderloos P., Lockie, R. J., & Chuttoorgoon, S. (1987). Field independence of students at Maharishi School of the Age of Enlightenment and a Montessori school. *Perceptual and Motor Skills* 65: 613–614.

http://www.globalcountry.org/wp/total-brain-
development/ Retrieved from http://
www.globalgoodnews.com/vedic-education/research.html

Greene, B. (2000). *The elegant universe. Superstrings,
hidden dimensions, and the quest for the ultimate theory.*
Vintage Series. New York: Random House.

Greene, B. (2004). *The fabric of the cosmos.* New York:
Random House.

Greene, B. (2011). Spooky action at a distance. PBS/
NOVA.

Grosswald, S. J., Stixrud, W. R., Travis, F., & Bateh, M.
A. (2008). Use of the Transcendental Meditation
technique to reduce symptoms of attention deficit
hyperactivity disorder (ADHD) by reducing stress and
anxiety: An exploratory study. In J.Norvilitis, (Ed.),
Current Issues in Education, [On-line], 10(2).

Grosswald, S.J. & Travis, F. (2011) ADHD and stress:
The role of meditation to reduce stress and improve brain
function and behavior regulation. In J.Norvilitis, (Ed.),
Current directions in ADHD and its treatment, 195-210.

Hagelin, J. S. (1987). Is consciousness the unified field?
A field theorist's perspective. *Modern Science and Vedic
Science,* 1(1): 29-87.

Hagelin, J. S. (1989). Restructuring physics from its
foundation in light of Maharishi's Vedic Science. *Modern
Science and Vedic Science,* 3(1): 3-72.

Hagelin, J.S. (1998). *Manual for a perfect government.*
Maharishi University of Management Press.

Harung, H.S. & Travis, F. (2012). Higher mind-brain
development in successful leaders: Testing a unified
theory of performance. *Cognitive Processing*, 13:
171-181.

Harung, H.F., Travis, F., Blank, W., & Heaton, D. (2009).
Higher development, brain integration, and excellence in
leadership. *Management Decision*, 47(6), 872-894.

Harung, H., Travis, F., Pensgaard, A. M., Boes, R., Cook-
Greuter, S., & Daley, K. (2011). Higher psycho-
physiological refinement in world-class Norwegian
athletes: Brain measures of performance capacity.
Scandinavian Journal of Exercise and Sport, 1, 32-41.

Heaton, D. & Travis, F. (2013). Consciousness, empathy,
and the brain. In K. Pavlovich and K. Krahnke (Eds.),
Organizing through empathy, pp. 17-33. Oxford, UK:
Routledge.

Hebert, R., Lehman, D., Tan, G., Travis, F., & Arenander,
A. (2005). Enhanced EEG alpha time-domain phase
synchrony during Transcendental Meditation:
Implications for cortical implication theory. *Signal
Processing*, 85 (11), 2213-2232.

Hjelle, L.A. (1974). Transcendental Meditation and
psychological health. *Perceptual and Motor Skills,* 39:
623-628.

James, W. (1899). *Human immortality: Two supposed objections to the doctrine.* Boston: Houghton, Mifflin & Co.

James, W. (1908). *The energies of men.* New York, Moffat, Yard and company.

James, W. (1910). *Varieties of religious experience.* New York: Vintage Books.

Jeans, J. (1981). *Physics and philosophy.* New York: Dover.

Jedraczak A. (1984). The Transcendental Meditation and TM-Sidhi program and field independence. *Perceptual and Motor Skills,* 59: 999-100.

Jevning, R., Wallace, R.K., & Beidebach, M. (1992). The physiology of meditation: A review. A wakeful hypometabolic integrated response. *Neuroscience and Biobehavioral Reviews* 16: 415-424.

Jibu, M., Hagan, S., Hameroff, S. R., Pribram, K. H., & Yasue, K. (1994). Quantum optical coherence in cytoskeletal microtubules; Implications for brain function. *BioSystems,* 32, 195-209.

Kanai, R., Feilden, T., Firth, C., & Rees, G. (2011). Political orientations are correlated with brain structures in young adults. *Current Biology,* 21(8): p.677-80.

Klein, D. B. (1984). *The concept of consciousness: A survey.* Lincoln: University of Nebraska Press.

Kuhn, T. (1962). *The structure of the scientific revolution.* (1st.ed.). Chicago: University of Chicago Press.

Lagrosen, Y., Travis, F., & Lagrosen, S. (2012). Brain integration as a driver for QM success. *International Journal of Quality and Service Sciences*, 4(3). 253-269.

Lappe, F. M. (1971). *Diet for a small planet.* New York: Ballantine Books, Inc.

Lappe, F.M. (2100). *EcoMind: Changing the way we think, to create the world we want.* New York: Nation Books.

Lappe, F. M. & Collins, J. (1977). *Food first: Beyond the myth of scarcity.* New York; Ballantine Books, Inc.

Luszczynska, A. & Schwarzer, R. (2005). Social cognitive theory. In M. Conner & P. Norman (Eds.), *Predicting health behaviour* (2nd ed. rev., pp. 127–169). Buckingham, England: Open University Press.

Lyubimov, N. N. (1992). Programme abstracts of the international symposium 'Consciousness and Brain'. Russian Academy of Sciences, Moscow. *globalgoodnews.com/vedic-education/research.html*

International Symposium on the Science of Creative Intelligence, (1971). MIU Press. Printed in Spain.

Maharishi Mahesh Yogi. (1966). *Science of being and art of living.* New York: Signet.

Maharishi Mahesh Yogi. (1972a). SCI Teacher Training Course, Maharishi International University.

Maharishi Mahesh Yogi. (1972b). SCI and the Environment. Videotaped lecture.

Maharishi Mahesh Yogi. (1986). *Maharishi's program to create world peace: Removing the basis of terrorism and war.* Washington, D. C.: Age of Enlightenment Press.

Maharishi Mahesh Yogi. (1990). *The Maharishi effect: Creating coherence in world consciousness. Promoting positive and evolutionary trends throughout the world: Results of scientific research.* Fairfield, Iowa: Maharishi International University Press.

Maharishi Mahesh Yogi. (1992). *Maharishi's absolute theory of government. Automation in administration.* The Netherlands: Maharishi Vedic University.

Mason, L., Alexander, C., Travis, F., Marsh, G., Orme-Johnson, D.W., Gackenback, J., Mason, D.C., Rainforth, M., & Walton, K.G. (1997). Electrophysiological correlates of higher states of consciousness during sleep in long-term practitioners of the Transcendental Meditation program. *Sleep*, 20: 102-110.

McEwen, B.S. (2006). Sleep deprivation as a neurobiolic and physiologic stressor: Allostasis and allostatic load. *Metabolism.* 55(10 Suppl 2); p. S20-3.

Nunez, P. (2010). *Brain, mind, and the structure of reality.* Cambridge, MA: Oxford University Press.

Orme-Johnson, D. W., Alexander, C. N., Davies, J. L., Chandler, H. M., & Larimore, W. E. (1988). International peace project in the Middle East: The effect of the Maharishi Technology of the Unified Field. *Journal of Conflict Resolution*, 32(4): 776-812.

Orme-Johnson, D. W., Cavanaugh, K. L., Alexander, C. N., Gelderloos, P., Dillbeck, M. C., Lanford, A. G., & Abou Nader, T. M. (1990). The influence of the Maharishi Technology of the Unified Field on world events and global social indicators: The effects of the Taste of Utopia Assembly. *Scientific research on Maharishi's Transcendental Meditation and TM-Sidhi Program: Collected papers, Volume. 4.* Vlodrop, Holland: Maharishi Vedic University Press.

Orme-Johnson, D. W., Dillbeck, M. C., Alexander, C. N., Chandler, H. M., & Cranson, R. W. (1989). Time series impact assessment analysis of reduced international conflict and terrorism: Effects of large assemblies of participants in the Transcendental Meditation and TM-Sidhi program. Presented at the 85th Annual Meeting of the American Political Science Association, Atlanta, Georgia. Also presented at the Annual Conference of the American Psychological Association, Boston, Massachusetts, 1990.

Orme-Johnson, D. W., Dillbeck, M. C., Bousquet, J. G., & Alexander, C. N. (1990). The World Peace Project of 1978: An experimental analysis of the application of the Maharishi Technology of the Unified Field in major world trouble spots. In *Scientific research on Maharishi's Transcendental Meditation and TM-Sidhi Program: Collected papers, Volume 4.* Vlodrop, Holland: Maharishi Vedic University Press.

Orme-Johnson, D. W. & Farrow, J.T. (Eds.). (1977). *Scientific Research on the Transcendental Meditation Programme: Collected papers, Volume 1.* Rheinweiler, Germany: MERU Press. (Papers 1–104).

Orme-Johnson, D.W., Gelderloos, P., & Dillbeck, M. C. (1988). The long-term effects of the Maharishi Technology of the Unified Field on the quality of life in the United States (1960 to 1984). *Social Science Perspectives Journal.*

Ormrod, J. E. (2006). *Educational psychology: Developing learners* (5th ed.). Upper Saddle River, N.J.: Pearson/Merrill Prentice Hall.

Pelletier, K. R. (1974). Influence of Transcendental Meditation upon autokinetic perception. *Perceptual and Motor Skills* 39: 1031–1034.

Rabinoff, R. A., Dillbeck, M. C., & Deissler, R (1981). Effect of coherent collective consciousness on the weather. *Scientific research on Maharishi's Transcendental Meditation and TM-Sidhi Program: Collected papers, Volume 4.* MUM Press.

Rotter, J. B. (1966). Generalized expectancies for internal versus external control of reinforcement. *Psychological Monographs: General & Applied,* 80(1) 1-28.

Schwartz, J. M. & Begley, S. (2002). *The mind and the brain: Neuroplasticity and the power of mental force.* Harper Collins Books: New York.

Tanner, M. A., Travis, F., Gaylord-King, C., Haaga, D. A. F., Grosswald, S., & Schneider, R. H. (2009). The effects of the Transcendental Meditation program on mindfulness. *Journal of Clinical Psychology.* 65(6), 574-589.

Travis, F. (2009). Brain functioning as the ground for spiritual experiences and ethical behavior. FBI Law Enforcement Bulletin, 78 (5), 26-32.

Travis F. (2011). Mindfulness and psychologic well-being: Are they related to type of meditation technique practiced? *The Journal of Alternative and Complementary Medicine*, 17(11): 983-4.

Travis, F. (2011). States of consciousness beyond waking, dreaming and sleeping: Perspectives from research on meditation experiences. In D. Certikovik & I. Cosvic (Eds.), *States of consciousness: Experimental insights into meditation, waking, sleep, and dreams.* The Frontiers Collection.

Travis, F. (2012). *Your brain is a river not a rock.* Fairfield: Total Brain Publications.

Travis, F. (2014). Transcendental experiences and meditation practice. Annuals of New York Academy of Science; *Advances in meditation research: Neuroscience and clinical applications,* 26, 295-298.

Travis F.T. (1990). An empirical test of Maharishi's junction point model of states of consciousness. *Modern Science and Vedic Science,* 4(1): 42-55.

Travis F.T. (1991). Eyes open and TM EEG patterns after one and after eight years of TM practice. *Psychophysiology,* 28 (3a): S58.

Travis, F.T. (1993). Respiratory, autonomic, and EEG correlates of transcendental consciousness experiences during Transcendental Meditation practice. *Society for Neuroscience Abstracts,* 18(1), 574.15.

Travis, F.T. (1994). The junction point model: A field model of waking, sleeping, and dreaming relating dream witnessing, the waking/sleeping transition, and Transcendental Meditation in terms of a common psychophysiologic state. *Dreaming,* 4(2): 91-104.

Travis, F.T. (1995). Within comparison of EEG and autonomic patterns during eyes-closed rest and transcendental meditation practice. *Psychophysiology* 32: S77.

Travis, F.T. (1996). Comparison of CNV amplitude and P300 latency and amplitude in subjects practicing the Transcendental Meditation technique for less than 1 year or more than 8 years. *Psychophysiology,* 33: S83.

Travis, F.T. (1998). Cortical and cognitive development in 4th, 8th, and 12th grade students: The contribution of speed of processing and executive functioning to cognitive development. *Biological Psychology*, 48, 37-56.

Travis, F.T. (2001). Autonomic and EEG patterns distinguish transcending from other experiences during Transcendental Meditation practice. *International Journal of Psychophysiology*, 42, 1-9.

Travis, F.T. (2004). Relationship between meditation practice and transcendent states of consciousness. *Biofeedback*, 32:3, 33-36.

Travis, F.T. (2005). The significance of transcendental consciousness for addressing the "hard" problem of consciousness. *Journal of Social Behavior and Personality,* 17, 123-135.

Travis, F. T. (2006). From I to I: Concepts of Self on an object-referral/Self-referral continuum. A. P. Prescott, (Ed.), *The concept of Self in psychology.* New York: Nova Publishing.

Travis, F.T. & Arenander, A. (2004). EEG asymmetry and mindfulness meditation. *Psychosomatic Medicine*, 66, 147-152.

Travis, F.T., Arenander, A., & DuBois, D. (2004). Psychological and physiological characteristics of a proposed object-referral/Self-referral continuum of Self-awareness. *Consciousness and Cognition*, 13/2, 401-420.

Travis, F.T. & Arenander, A. (2006). Cross-sectional and longitudinal study of effects of Transcendental Meditation practice on frontal power asymmetry and frontal coherence. *International Journal of Neuroscience*, 116 (11): 1519-1538.

Travis, F. & Brown, S. (2009). My brain made me do it: Brain maturation and levels of Self-development. In A. H. Pfaffenberger, P.W. Marko, & T. Greening (Eds.), *The postconventional personality: Perspectives on higher development.* New York: Sage Publishing.

Travis, F. Grosswald, S., & Stixrud, W. (2011). ADHD, brain functioning and Transcendental Meditation practice. *Mind and Brain: The Journal of Psychiatry*, 2 (1), 73-81.

Travis, F., Haaga, D.H., Hagelin, J., Tanner, M., Nidich, S., Gaylord-King, C., Grosswald, S., Rainforth, M., & Schneider, R. (2009). Effects of Transcendental Meditation practice on brain functioning and stress reactivity in college students. *International Journal of Psychophysiology,* 71, 170-176.

Travis, F., Haaga, D.H., Hagelin, J., Tanner, M., Arenander, A., Nidich, S., Gaylord-King, C., Grosswald, S., Rainforth, M., & Schneider, R. (2010). A Self-referral default brain state: Patterns of coherence, power, and eLORETA sources during eyes-closed rest and the Transcendental Meditation practice. *Cognitive Processes*, 11(1), 21-30.

Travis, F., Harung, H., & Lagrosen, Y. (2011). Moral development, peak experiences and brain patterns in professional and amateur classical musicians: Support for a unified theory of performance. *Consciousness and Cognition*, 20, 1256-1264.

Travis, F. & Lagrosen, Y. (2014). Creativity and brain functioning in product development engineers: A canonical correlation analysis. *Creativity Research Journal*, 26 (2), 239-243.

Travis, F.T. & Miskov, S. (1994). P300 latency and amplitude after eyes-closed rest and after transcendental meditation practice. *Psychophysiology*, 31: S98.

Travis F.T. & Orme-Johnson D.W. (1989). Field model of consciousness: EEG coherence changes as indicators of field effects. *International Journal of Neuroscience*, 49: 203-211.

Travis, F.T. & Pearson, C. (2000). Distinct phenomenological and physiological correlates of 'consciousness itself.' *International Journal of Neuroscience*, 100, 77-89.

Travis, F. & Shear, J. (2010). Focused attention, open monitoring, and automatic self-transcending: Categories to organize meditations from Vedic, Buddhist, and Chinese traditions. *Consciousness and Cognition*, 19: 1110-1119.

Travis, F.T., Tecce, J., Arenander, A., & Wallace, R.K. (2002). Patterns of EEG coherence, power, and contingent negative variation characterize the integration of transcendental and waking states. *Biological Psychology*, 61, 293-319.

Travis, F.T., Tecce, J., & Durchholz, C. (2001). Cortical plasticity, CNV, and transcendent experiences: Replication with subjects reporting permanent transcendental experiences. *Psychophysiology,* 38, suppl: S95.

Travis, F.T., Tecce, J.J., & Guttman, J. (2000). Cortical plasticity, contingent negative variation, and transcendent experiences during practice of the Transcendental Meditation technique. *Biological Psychology*, 55, 41-55.

Travis, F.T. & Wallace R.K. (1997) Autonomic patterns during respiratory suspensions: Possible markers of transcendental consciousness. *Psychophysiology*, 34: 39-46.

Travis, F.T. & Wallace R.K. (1999). EEG and autonomic patterns during eyes-closed rest and Transcendental Meditation practice: The basis for a neural model of TM practice. *Consciousness and Cognition*, 8, 302-318.

Wallace, R. K. Neurophysiology of enlightenment. Paper presented at the 26th International Congress of Physiological Sciences, New Delhi, India, October 1974. Livingston Manor, New York: MIU Press, 1974.

Wallace, R. K. The physiology of higher states of consciousness. Paper presented at the Conference on Higher States of Consciousness: Theoretical and Experimental Perspectives, Chicago, August, 1991.

Wallace, R.K. & Benson, H. (1971). A wakeful hypometabolic physiologic state. *The American Journal of Physiology.*

Wallace, R.K., Orme-Johnson, D.W., & Dillbeck. M. C. (Eds.). (1990). *Scientific research on Maharishi's Transcendental Meditation and TM-Sidhi Program: Collected papers, Volume 5.* Fairfield, Iowa, USA: MIU Press. (Papers 356–430).

Witkin, H.A. & Asch, S. E. (1948). Studies in space orientation: IV. Further experiments on perception of the upright with displaced visual fields. *Journal of Experimental Psychology,* 38(6), 762-782.

World Peace Group: Mozambique Transformation.(1992). Retrieved from http://www.worldpeacegroup.org Mozambique_transformation.html

CREATING AN IDEAL WORLD

SCI & ECO-MIND

ECO-MIND.	ENLIGHTENED-MIND.
MENTAL MAP.	BRAIN MAP.
SEE THE WORLD THROUGH A FILTER OR LENS.	SEE THE WORLD THROUGH A WIDE-ANGLE LENS. ENHANCED PERCEPTION IN HIGHER STATES OF CONSCIOUSNESS.
WE DON'T SEE THINGS AS THEY ARE. WE SEE THINGS AS WE ARE.	THE WORLD IS AS WE ARE. KNOWLEDGE IS STRUCTURED IN CONSCIOUSNESS. KNOWLEDGE IS DIFFERENT IN DIFFERENT STATES OF CONSCIOUSNESS.
NOT ENOUGH GOODS OR GOODNESS.	ALL GOOD EVERYWHERE. NON-GOOD NOWHERE.
IMPORTANCE OF IDEAS. WAKING STATE MODEL OF ENVIRONMENTAL CHANGE.	IMPORTANCE OF TRANSCENDING THE THINKING PROCESS. EXPERIENCE HIGHER STATES OF CONSCIOUSNESS TO EFFECTIVELY CREATE ENVIRONMENTAL CHANGE.
SEPARATENESS. SCARCITY.	UNITY. INTEGRATION. ABUNDANCE.
PESSIMISM. NOTHING IS POSSIBLE.	CONSCIOUSNESS IS A FIELD OF ALL POSSIBILITIES. EVERYTHING AND ANYTHING IS POSSIBLE.

ENGAGED IN PROBLEM SOLVING.	SCI OFFERS THE SOLUTION TO ALL PROBLEMS.
POWERLESSNESS.	MAN IS MASTER OF HIS OWN DESTINY. INCREASED SELF-EFFICACY, FIELD INDEPENDENCE, AND LOCUS OF CONTROL.
MISALIGNMENT WITH OUR OWN NATURE AND THE WIDER LAWS OF NATURE.	SELF-REFERRAL AWARENESS. SPONTANEOUS RIGHT ACTION ALIGNED WITH ALL THE LAWS OF NATURE.
LIFE-DAMAGING PRACTICES.	LIFE-SUPPORTING SOLUTIONS.
THOUGHT TRAPS VERSUS THOUGHT LEAPS.	TRANSCEND THOUGHT. LEAP BEYOND THOUGHT TO THE UNBOUNDED SOURCE OF THOUGHT.
WHY DO WE CREATE A SOCIAL ECOLOGY WHICH IS DESTRUCTIVE FOR THE PLANET?	EDUCATION MUST TRAIN CITIZENS HOW NOT TO VIOLATE THE LAWS OF NATURE.
LIVING DEMOCRACY. GOVERNMENT GOVERNS FOR THE PUBLIC GOOD.	AUTOMATION IN ADMINISTRATION. THE ADMINISTERED ADMINISTERS THE ADMINISTRATION.
THIN DEMOCRACY MIS-ALIGNED WITH NATURE.	IDEAL ADMINISTRATION ALIGNED WITH NATURAL LAW.
WE MUST INTERACT WITH THE ENVIRONMENT TO CHANGE THE ENVIRONMENT.	ACTION AT A DISTANCE. QUANTUM ENTANGLEMENT.

THE ENVIRONMENT IS PERCEIVED AS SOMETHING OUTSIDE OF OURSELF.	WE CREATE/CHOOSE THE ENVIRONMENT WE WANT. OUR BRAIN CREATES THE WORLD WE WANT. IN HIGHER STATES OF CONSCIOUSNESS ENVIRONMENT IS A WAVE OF THE SELF.
THINK LIKE AN ECO-MIND.	TRANSCEND THINKING. TRANSCEND THE CONSCIOUS CAPACITY OF THE MIND. UNFOLD TOTAL BRAIN POTENTIAL. LIVE HIGHER STATES OF CONSCIOUSNESS. THINK FROM THE FULLY EXPANDED LEVEL OF THE ENLIGHTENED-MIND.